COLOR FOR HEALING

Harnessing the therapeutic powers of the rainbow
for health and well-being, with over 150 photographs

LILIAN VERNER-BONDS

LORENZ BOOKS

This edition is published by Lorenz Books,
an imprint of Anness Publishing Ltd,
108 Great Russell Street, London, WC1B 3NA
info@anness.com

www.lorenzbooks.com; www.annesspublishing.com

If you like the images in this book and would like to investigate using them
for publishing, promotions or advertising, please visit our website
www.practicalpictures.com for more information.

Publisher: Joanna Lorenz
Managing Editor: Helen Sudell
Project Editor: Emma Gray
Additional material: Sue and Simon Lilly, and Sally Morningstar
Designer: Jane Coney
Photographer: Don Last
Illustrator: Giovanna Pierce
Production Controller: Mai-Ling Collyer

Publisher's note:
The reader should not regard the recommendations, ideas and techniques expressed
and described in this book as substitutes for the advice of a qualified medical practitioner
or other qualifed professional. Any use to which the recommendations, ideas and
techniques are put is at the reader's sole discretion and risk.

contents

introduction

On a purely instinctive level, we choose the colours of our clothes, paints and decor in the home, even the food we eat, to reflect our mood and emotions; this can be seen as colour healing in its simplest form. By exploring the subject on a more subtle level, however, we can also use colour healing to treat specific ailments, or to create a particular atmosphere suitable for the purpose of a room, whether calm and relaxing or lively and energizing. So, go ahead – follow your instinct – read this book and find out how you can enhance your health and wellbeing.

Life in colour

You are swamped with colour from the moment you are born: it is an aspect of everything you eat, drink, touch and are surrounded by. You can use colours to describe your health, attitudes, emotions and even your spiritual or psychic experiences. Nearly everyone takes colour for granted most of the time, but it is impossible to be indifferent to it. Colour affects every environment: at home, at work, at school, in the city or in the countryside. The colours of the clothes you wear affects your mood and reflects your personality, which in turn influences other people's perception of you and so affects your relationships.

Colour helps you to determine when fruits are ripe. Your skin changes colour with shock, shyness or excitement. Too much yellow light can cause arguments between people, and blue light can quieten them. Colour constantly enriches your life, whether it is the green of grass or trees, deep blue sky, a purple and gold sunset, or a beautiful rainbow.

Without light there is no life, and no growth. A plant deprived of light will soon wither and die and living beings are continually reacting to the wide range of stimuli called light. From light come all the colours, each with its own impact upon living systems. Light is energy, and all energy acts upon everything with which it comes into contact. What you see as colour is simply the brain's way of recognizing the different energy qualities of light.

Many healing needs can be met by the use of colour to bring about harmony and balance within the psyche and the body. The invisible vibrations of colour can either relax or stimulate,

◄ CHILDREN ARE ATTRACTED BY THE STRENGTH OF BRIGHT COLOURS.

▲ Colour enriches your life. Many cultures use bright colours when celebrating special occasions.

home can be a haven of health and peace when you decorate and furnish it in colours appropriate to your needs and aspirations.

Disease is often regarded as an enemy, but think of it as your friend. It is telling you the truth about yourself, and the ways in which you are out of harmony with the "real" you. Working with colour and understanding the connection between yourself and colour offers a key to good health and vitality.

according to the colours chosen for healing. Its power is both transcendent and intuitive, and there are several ways of harnessing it for health and well-being. Colour does more than just please the eye. You can eat it, drink it, and wear appropriately coloured clothes or jewellery, absorbing the colour through your skin as well as your eyes. Your

Although colour healing can be very effective, it should not replace any medical treatment. If any illness persists, or the symptoms become worse, consult a qualified doctor or health professional.

▼ The beautiful colours of the sunset are joyous and calming.

The evolution of colour healing

Ancient cultures worshipped the sun – whence all light, and all colour, comes – and were aware of its healing powers. The therapeutic use of colour can be traced in the teachings attributed to the Egyptian god Thoth.

EARLY COLOUR THERAPY

Following the ancient teachings, Egyptian and Greek physicians – including Hippocrates, the father of Western medicine – used different coloured ointments and salves as remedies, and practised in treatment rooms painted in healing shades. In 1st-century Rome, the physician Aulus Cornelius Celsus wrote about the therapeutic use of colour, but with the coming of Christianity such ancient wisdom came to be associated with pagan beliefs and was disallowed by the Church.

In the 9th century the Arab physician Avicenna systematized the teachings of Hippocrates. He wrote about colour as a symptom of disease and as a treatment, suggesting, for example, that red would act as a stimulant on blood flow while yellow could reduce pain and inflammation. However, by the 18th century philosophers and scientists were more concerned with the material world, and insisted on visible proof of scientific theories.

▼ THE ANCIENT EGYPTIANS KNEW ABOUT THE HEALING PROPERTIES OF COLOURS.

◀ Bathe yourself in a natural green vibration to instil positive thoughts and creativity.

establishment's continued scepticism, therapists have since developed the use of colour in both psychological testing and physical diagnosis. The Lüscher Colour Test is based on the theory that colours stimulate different parts of the autonomic nervous system, affecting metabolic rate and glandular secretions, and studies in the 1950s showed that yellow and red light raised blood pressure while blue light tended to lower it. The use of blue light to treat neonatal jaundice is now common practice, and it has also been effective as pain relief in cases of rheumatoid arthritis.

Advances in medicine focused on surgery and drugs, and less quantifiable healing techniques that dealt with spiritual and mental wellbeing were rejected.

Colour therapy rediscovered

In 1878 Edwin Babbitt published *The Principles of Light and Colour* and achieved world renown with his comprehensive theory, prescribing colours for a range of conditions. Despite the medical

▶ Green, turquoise and blue objects have a tranquil air.

Natural colour

From forests to cities, people adapt to the unique qualities of their surroundings. Colour creates the ambience of a place because the vibrational energy of colour operates directly on your energy levels and emotions.

THE CALM OF NATURE

Most people experience a lifting of mood on a woodland walk as the green of nature fills their vision. The effects of colour can be felt when relaxing by the sea in summer, the predominant colours being the blues of the sea and sky, which generate a feeling of expansiveness and peace.

Turquoise is an important colour that tempers the deeper blues with an extra sense of calmness and comfort. The golden yellow of sand and sunlight energizes and balances the body's systems, reducing anxiety and stress levels.

▲ THE STRIKING COLOURS OF THE PEACOCK'S TAIL FEATHERS ACT AS A TERRITORIAL WARNING SIGNAL TO ITS COMPETITORS.

THE SEEING WORLD

Full colour vision is a rare development in the animal world; it occurs in the higher vertebrates – including humans – as well as a few unexpected animals, such as the tortoise and the octopus.

Striking colour displays are used by many animals, such as the peacock, to attract mates or to deter enemies. Using colour as camouflage is also common. The squid has a complex language of expression, sending waves of colours across its body.

◀ THE BLUE OF THE SEA IS ONE OF THE MOST SOOTHING COLOURS OF ALL.

Colours in different cultures

Colour is an intrinsic part of human life, and although the physical effects of colour are biologically constant, its psychological interpretation and symbolism can vary when it forms part of a cultural language.

RED

In Tibetan and some pagan traditions, red is the colour of the female sun, white the male moon. The two symbolize the union of opposites: the power of creation. Red can also be associated with the male, for example Santa Claus, who also retains the symbolism of the Arctic shaman bringing healing and gifts to his people.

GREEN

In the Western tradition, green is associated with wild nature, the power of growth and uncultivated space inhabited by spirits, elves

▾ IN TIBET, RED IS A COLOUR ASSOCIATED WITH CREATIVITY, PRAYER AND HEALING.

▲ WHITE CAN BE SYMBOLIC OF PURITY AND INNOCENCE, AND SO IT IS OFTEN CHOSEN AS THE COLOUR FOR BRIDAL WEAR.

and fairies. In the world of Islam, the colour green is sacred. In a landscape dominated by arid wilderness, green represents the oasis, the sign of life, water and shelter: the symbol of paradise.

BLACK AND WHITE

In much of Europe death has been associated with black. In China, however, white is seen as the colour of winter, when all things return to a dormant state, so mourners wear white. Chinese people tend to avoid wearing white in everyday life because it reminds them of a shroud, whereas in the West white is associated simply with purity.

Colour at home

Colour is a sensation that enriches the world: there is no better way to use it than by harnessing its strength and benefits to enhance your home. Blending colours successfully can help to create a harmonious atmosphere.

WELCOMING THE SUN

When you are creating your home environment, take into consideration the amount of sunlight in each room. It is important that the glow from the sun's beams is received into your psyche, for its purifying effect. Allowing sunlight to flood into dark corners also rids a room of its staleness and kills some bacteria.

When you are decorating, think about the effects of colour, how the room will be used, and also about the people who will use it: do they have any problems that could be alleviated or worsened by your colour choices? What are their ambitions and aims?

COLOUR AND SIZE

Take into consideration the size and shape of each room: the stronger the colour, the smaller a room will seem. Small rooms tend to look more spacious decorated in single pale colours. Colours become more intense in larger areas, and a strong colour can enclose a room, causing claustrophobia. Dark narrow rooms need light, clear colours.

Check how much daylight the space gets before using white, as a bright white room can be tiring for the eyes and cause frustration. Deep colours may look good with the sun on them; they become several shades duller at night in artificial light, but can look cosy if firelight or candlelight are used. If you are painting only one wall in a different colour, do not choose a wall where there is a door or window as this dissipates the colour energy.

◄ AN ORANGE ROOM WILL INSTIL CHEERFULNESS INTO ITS OCCUPANTS.

Room-by-room guide to colour

The colours of your home should suit not only the function of each room, but should also be used to create harmony. Use coloured flowers or ornaments for particular occasions to influence the atmosphere.

Entrance hall: To welcome your guests include warm colours, such as the range of reds. Or to create a sense of space choose softer pastel shades.

Kitchen: Too much green may slow you down just when you need to be active, but a touch of yellow inspires efficiency.

Living room: Yellow puts people in a good humour; add brown to give a sense of security.

Dining room: Include a hint of silver at a dinner party. It aids digestion and is uplifting – adding sparkle to guests' conversations.

Bedroom: Calming blue is a perfect colour for the bedroom. A touch of indigo can also help if  you suffer from headaches or insomnia. Stimulating red may cause sleeplessness, so avoid.

Bathroom: Hints of pale green will soothe and feed a tired nervous system.

Colour at work

Until quite recently, coloured decor for offices was almost unthinkable. Sterile white, grey or drab browns were the norm. Today, the trend is to make the most of the effect that colour has on people and the ambience it can create.

THE EFFECT OF COLOUR

Promoting the effective use of colour in the office is important both for the comfort of the employees and the productivity of the business. If thoughtlessly applied, colour can interfere and distract from work. If only white is used it can cause frustration. Blue creates an atmosphere of calm and is good for creativity. Brown creates tiredness and lethargy and grey induces depression and melancholy. If you use beige, add green or rose pink to alleviate the negative slackness that it can bring to the room.

Don't forget details such as company stationery, as it also makes a colour statement. You could change from white paper to a shade that may better reflect your company's image.

THE CITY OFFICE

Offices in which activity is high, in areas such as sales and banking, should use red upholstery. This definitely puts workers in the hot seat and adds impetus and drive to their performance. Add green walls, to counteract the red and reduce headaches that are brought on by the pressure of work.

◄ BLUE IN THE STUDY AREA CREATES A SENSE OF CALM AND CAN INSPIRE THE WRITER.

THE EXECUTIVE OFFICE

When you are the boss you need an office where employees and directors can talk to you and be reminded that you lead the way. A purple carpet gives an impression of big ideas and creativity along with luxury and authority. Touches of gold encourage feelings of trust and loyalty, but don't forget to add healthy green plants to represent money and to balance power and character.

THE OPEN-PLAN OFFICE

When choosing colours for a large office, you would be well advised to make the overall decor a basic cream and introduce touches of brighter colours, such as orange, emerald green, rose and rich blue. If only one accent colour can be used, choose a bright turquoise as this will help to give a greater sense of privacy.

THE HOME OFFICE

An office at home can encourage the workaholic. An effective combination would be a royal blue carpet with yellow curtains and pale blue or primrose yellow walls: this should succeed in keeping the business in the office only, and not allow work to penetrate into your personal life.

◀ GREEN IN THE OFFICE WILL HELP TO GENERATE ABUNDANCE AND MAKE MONEY.

Light waves and colour

Visible light is a small portion of the electromagnetic spectrum, which also includes ultraviolet and infrared light. These last two are just beyond the vision of humans, but can still have an effect on our health.

LIGHT WAVES

The distance between the two crests of a wave (the wavelength) determines what type of wave it is. Radio waves are very long; cosmic rays are very short. Around the middle of the spectrum is the tiny portion we experience as visible light. Within this, further gradations produce different colours. The longest waves are at the red end of the spectrum, and the shortest waves are at the purple end, with those of the other colours falling in between. Colour therapists often refer to pure colours as "rays".

◀ WHITE LIGHT REFRACTED THROUGH A PRISM REVEALS ITS COMPONENT COLOURS – THE FULL RAINBOW SPECTRUM.

WHAT IS COLOUR?

A coloured surface absorbs or reflects certain wavelengths of light. A red flower absorbs all light striking it except the red end of the spectrum, which is reflected. A white surface reflects all light that hits it, while a black surface absorbs it all.

The emotional and physiological response of humans to colour is profound: even people without sight will identify warm and cool colours. The stimulating effects of reds and oranges and the calming qualities of blues and violets, for example, are linked to the biological triggers of daylight and nightfall, and these [responses] are harnessed in colour healing.

◀ A RAINBOW IS WHITE LIGHT REFRACTED OR SEPARATED INTO ITS COMPONENT COLOURS.

Sense of sight

Colour has been shown to initiate profound changes in the nervous system. The eyes allow the light energy of colour to be carried to the centre of the brain, influencing cellular function, physical activity, emotional and mental states.

THE EYE

The human eye is a sophisticated sensing device. Light passes through the transparent lens and stimulates the specialized light-sensitive cells in the retina at the back of the eyeball. These send electrical impulses via the optic nerve into the brain to be interpreted. The process of vision is primarily a function of the brain, for the eyes "see" only a small area at any one time. The eyeballs move very rapidly across the field of vision, 50–70 times a second, and the visual part of the brain makes sense of all the information.

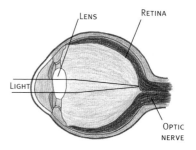

▲ LIGHT ENTERS THE EYE, TRIGGERING THE NERVES IN THE LIGHT-SENSITIVE CELLS IN THE RETINA, WHICH THEN LINK UP TO THE BRAIN.

COLOUR AND THE BRAIN

Nerves go directly from the retina to the hypothalamus and pituitary gland (both are parts of the brain), which control most of the body's life-sustaining functions, and modify behaviour patterns and regulate energy levels. Thus the application of light can directly influence the body.

In addition, specialist cells within the skin have a sensitivity to light and so this is a second area in which your body can be directly influenced by colour.

◀ SOME CREATURES CAN SEE A WIDER SPECTRUM OF COLOURS THAN HUMANS.

The psychology of colour

Colour can affect your personality whether this is due to cultural conditioning or personal associations. If you were wearing blue on a very happy occasion, for example, the colour may continue to remind you of that experience.

COLOUR AND MOOD

There are psychological associations with each colour, and colours can be linked with moods. Reds, oranges and yellows are warm and expansive and give a feeling of energy, excitement and joy. Blues, indigos and purples are calming and cool. They quieten the temperament and induce relaxation. The psychology of colour is a language that you can learn, just as you can learn to read and write. When you understand the basic meanings of colours you can choose the colours in your life according to your needs.

▲ THE SUNSET COLOURS, PINK AND GOLD, ARE NURTURING AND EXCELLENT FOR HEALING EMOTIONAL TRAUMA.

RESTORING BALANCE

Each colour vibrates at a distinctive rate that corresponds with a part of the body. When you are well you may like most colours, but illness will bring out preferences for specific colours. It is these that are needed for healing. When you are exhausted you may be drawn to reds. Some-one who is over-excited would benefit from blues, but depression needs yellows and golds.

The following guide will help you to explore how you feel, and help you to choose colours to enhance your wellbeing.

◀ RED IS THE COLOUR ASSOCIATED WITH ADVENTURE SPORTS SUCH AS SKI-ING.

Chakras and colour

Ancient texts describe seven energy centres, or chakras, arranged along the spinal column. Each one focuses energy, and each is associated with a colour. They are forever changing and balancing to preserve your wellbeing.

WORKING WITH CHAKRAS

Every individual has a particular chakra pattern, some being more dominant than others. This can lead to an energy imbalance, so you will need to determine which chakras need balancing. In this way you will be able to maintain a harmonious and healthy state.

Colour therapy is a technique that can work directly with chakras. Shining coloured light on the chakra, over the whole body or through the eyes all create physical, emotional and mental changes which re-balance the chakras. If coloured light is not easily available, visualizing the necessary colours can also work.

THE SEVEN CHAKRAS

CROWN CHAKRA: purple
Overall balance, intuition.
Linked to pineal gland.

BROW CHAKRA: indigo
Understanding, perception.
Linked to pituitary gland.

THROAT CHAKRA: blue
Communication, expression.
Linked to thyroid glands.

HEART CHAKRA: green
Relationships, development.
Linked to heart and thymus.

SOLAR PLEXUS CHAKRA: yellow
Sense of identity, confidence.
Linked to pancreas and spleen.

SACRAL CHAKRA: orange
Creativity, feelings, sex drive.
Linked to adrenal glands.

BASE CHAKRA: red
Survival, stability, practicality.
Linked to gonads.

▼ THE POSITION AND COLOUR OF CHAKRAS (ENERGY CENTRES) ON THE BODY.

The energy of brilliance

Brilliance represents the universal intelligence and its source is the sun. Created when all rays of colour come together in perfect balance, it is the light from which all colours spring: the light seen in near-death experiences.

THE CHARACTER OF BRILLIANCE

Brilliance itself is not a colour: it is the original or cosmic light. Add a touch of brilliance to any colour and it will become brighter. Without brilliance there can be no vision. Brilliance cuts directly through to the truth. It is the hard light that exposes all flaws and

▸ BRILLIANCE SURROUNDS THE WHOLE BODY.

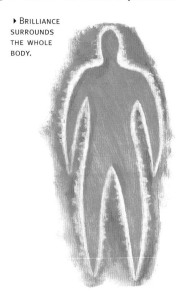

corruption. It contains the essence of all qualities, both positive and negative, sparkling in the brilliance of perfection. It clears the way for necessary actions. Brilliance clears any cloudiness in a person or over-dominance of any one colour. To recharge yourself at any time simply visualize pure brilliant

◂ BATHING IN A WATERFALL IS LIKE STANDING IN A CASCADE OF BRILLIANT LIGHT.

▶ This arrangement of six clear crystals is called the Seal of Solomon. It will quieten your mind and inspire brilliant insights.

light. When you say that someone is "brilliant", you are really acknowledging his or her purity of vision and action.

Brilliance and the body

The lymphatic system and the tissues that filter out the debris from the body relate to brilliance. Crystal clear water is pure liquid brilliance: bathing in a waterfall is the equivalent of standing under a cascade of clear light. Another

way to apply brilliance to yourself is to stand in front of an open window, or to go outside and take a brief sunshine bath: you can renew yourself time and time again.

WHEN BRILLIANCE CAN HELP

• Brilliance will bring a ray of hope to your life when all seems lost. • It can also bring change, and allows the delusions of your life to dissolve. You will see situations clearly and it will allow you to wipe the slate clean. • Applying brilliance may bring about a move to a new home, a change of job, or a subtle inner transformation. You will find that old patterns fall away and are replaced with new ones, full of joy and an uplifting of the spirit.

▶ Brilliance captured in clear crystals inspires clear thoughts.

The energy of red

Red is the nearest visible light to infrared. It is a fiery force: the spirit of physical life, full of power and drive. It signifies courage and liberation, passion and excitement. Too much red burns, but at the right level it supports life.

THE CHARACTER OF RED

When the influence of red is managed well within the system, its energy can be harnessed to motivate people. These are the innovators and entrepreneurs who are full of ideas. They prefer to move from one project to another, getting things started and then moving on.

People under the influence of red are often renowned for their daring exploits and can be somewhat extrovert and boastful about their skills. An overload of red causes restlessness and impatience in those nearby. It can result in selfishness, making people focus on their own needs and survival above everything else. Sometimes this drive to survive is what fuels

▲ A BRIGHT RED SKY AT SUNRISE CAN SIGNIFY THE APPROACH OF A CHANGEABLE AND STORMY WEATHER SYSTEM.

impulsive actions and rash comments. Red at its worst is tyrannical, seeking advancement no matter who or what suffers.

At its best, red will ensure a satisfying and passionate love life. Red brings focus to the physicality of life, to the process of living.

◄ FOR AN EXCITING DAY, DRESS YOUR CHILD IN RED CLOTHES.

CAUTION
Do not use red lighting in chromotherapy above the waist for heart conditions. Medical advice should be taken regarding any heart problem.

◀ RED IS THE COLOUR OF THE BASE CHAKRA, THE AREA WHICH GOVERNS REPRODUCTION.

The colour red is symbolic of what you need to survive. Life should be grabbed and lived with a sense of immediacy. Without red you may become listless and out of touch with reality.

RED AND THE BODY

Primarily, red is associated with the genitals and reproductive organs. Another area of red focus is the blood and circulation, as it increases the body's ability to absorb iron. Red also prompts the release of adrenalin into the bloodstream – hence its connection with aggression.

WHEN RED CAN HELP

• Use red to help circulatory problems, such as cold hands and feet, hardening of the arteries, anaemia and exhaustion. • Red can also be used to treat infertility and is especially good for stiff muscles and joints, particularly in the legs and feet.
• Red is useful in cases of paralysis, and works excellently if also combined with physiotherapy (physical therapy). • Red counteracts shyness and enables you to put your life back into action.

Red is a colour charged with energy and vitality. After an illness, when the body has been weakened, red is excellent for stimulating renewed strengths and encouraging recovery.

◀ THE LAVA FLOW FROM VOLCANOES IS RED. IT IS NATURE'S WARNING SIGNAL FOR DANGER.

The energy of orange

As a mixture of red and yellow, orange blends the properties of both colours. Orange energy displays some sense of direction and purpose – it moves along those pathways that fuel its own existence.

THE CHARACTER OF ORANGE

Orange has a persistent nature and can be summed up by one word: opportunity. Always one jump ahead, orange has the courage to grasp opportunities as soon as they occur. Orange is a strong colour that dares to trust intuition, tapping into creative resources and allowing skills to develop. The orange personality loves to experiment with new and exciting recipes in the kitchen. They are physical and will be drawn to sports of any kind.

▼ THE FLAMES OF A FIRE SHOW THE MANY DIFFERENT SHADES OF ORANGE.

▸ THIS GINGER KITTEN WILL GROW UP TO BE BRAVE, FRIENDLY AND FULL OF FUN.

Curiosity is one of the driving characteristics of the orange vibration and this brings with it exploration and creativity, particularly on practical physical levels. It tests, then accepts or rejects. It has impetus, self-reliance and practical knowledge.

Orange strength is subtle – it stimulates gently. It broadens life and is very purposeful. Orange breaks down barriers and gives the courage to make changes and face the consequences, good or bad. Because the orange energy is purposeful and has an instinct for moving on, it can creatively remove those blocks that cause restriction and stagnation.

The orange personality is genial, optimistic, tolerant, benign and warm-hearted, believing in friendship and community. The unkind practical joker is negative

▶ Orange is the colour of the sacral chakra and governs the gut instincts.

It governs the gut instincts and it enables you to become aware of the needs of your physical body.

▲ Boost a party atmosphere by adding orange decorations to enhance communication between guests.

orange. A balance of orange energy brings a willingness to get involved; it gives you the ability to fill your time creatively.

Orange and the body
The lower back, lower intestines, the kidneys, adrenal glands and abdomen are all linked to orange.

▼ In the flower world, orange represents the doctor.

When orange can help

• Grief, bereavement and loss can all be treated with orange. Orange vibrations will bring you through the shock of deep outrage and will give added strength where it is needed to pull through adversity. • It can also be useful when there is an inability to let go of the past. Orange removes the inhibitions and psychological paralysis that occur when people are afraid of moving forwards in their life. • Orange can help with the fear of enjoying sensual pleasure, it can relieve over-seriousness, a feeling of bleakness and boredom, or a lack of interest in the world outside.
• Orange can be used to treat asthma, bronchitis, epilepsy, mental disorders, rheumatism, torn ligaments, aching and broken bones.

The energy of yellow

Yellow is the brightest colour of the spectrum. Its sunny hue brings clarity of thought, warmth and vitality. Yellow pinpoints issues and leaves no stone unturned in its search for understanding.

THE CHARACTER OF YELLOW

The yellow vibration is concerned with discrimination and decision-making, both skills which are constantly needed for physical and mental wellbeing. Yellow is the colour of the scientist. It unravels problems and focuses the attention, loves new ideas and is flexible and highly adaptable. Yellow has no hesitation; it decides quickly and acts at once. It smartens the reflexes.

Yellow is the great communicator and a favourite pastime is networking. It has financial

▲ YELLOW REPRESENTS MENTAL VIGOUR AND CAN GIVE YOU ENERGY WHEN YOU NEED IT.

ambition – though holding on to money may be difficult. Yellow has the ability to get things done. It has self-control, style and plenty of sophistication.

▼ YELLOW SWEEPS AWAY CONFUSION AND HELPS YOU THINK CLEARLY.

SHADES OF YELLOW

As with all colours, different hues of yellow will create markedly different responses. Pale primrose yellow is associated with great spirituality, questioning the world beyond, whereas a clean, clear yellow empties the mind and keeps it alert. Acid yellow can promote feelings of suspicion and negative criticism, and a tendency to bear grudges and resentment.

▲ Surrounding yourself with yellow can help to enhance your sense of self-esteem and self-worth.

Yellow broadcasts a feeling of wellbeing and self-confidence. People feel good around those under the yellow ray. They are sunny and willing, unless they are upset, when they can be acid and sharp-tongued.

Yellow and the body

The colour yellow is connected to the pancreas, liver, skin, solar plexus, spleen, gall bladder, stomach

◄ Yellow is the colour of the solar plexus chakra, and governs the stomach.

When yellow can help

• Use yellow when you need to enliven a sluggish system: it will help to clear away toxins and stimulate the flow of gastric juices so improving nutrient digestion. • It can also be used to treat menopausal flushes, menstrual difficulties and other hormonal problems.

• Yellow is the great eliminator that clears toxins from your system. So apply if you are suffering from frequent minor illnesses, intolerances and allergies or constipation.

• Feelings of lethargy and depression brought on by dull weather respond well to a dose of yellow light, which can also help improve a poor memory or an inability to study. • Yellow can help to improve self-esteem, and reduce negativity and anxiety.

• In cases of diabetes, rheumatism and anorexia nervosa, yellow can sometimes help to relieve the symptoms associated with the illness.

and nervous system. Both the immune system and the digestive system rely on yellow to keep the gastric juices flowing. This colour helps to clear blockages of all kinds.

The energy of green

The colour green is found midway in the spectrum. It is made up of two colours: yellow and blue. Yellow brings wisdom and clarity while blue promotes peace. Green's basic qualities are balance and harmony.

THE CHARACTER OF GREEN

Whereas reds, oranges and yellows are warm, and blues, indigo and violets are cool, green can be either. Green aids the memory, which makes it an important healing colour. Most physical and mental illnesses result from events in the past. Green can release these traumas.

Green is the colour of the plant kingdom. It stands for growth and therefore change, since life is a process of transformation from one state to another. Growth needs balance and order for it to be sustainable, with each stage acting as a foundation for the next.

Green energy has to do with the pushing back of boundaries, of growing beyond what is known. Because green is connected to the heart it must develop relationships with the things around it, but it also needs a degree of control and power, which may be supportive or destructive. Positive green is the giver: sensible, socially aware, helpful and selfless. Green is about finding self-awareness which helps to bring self-acceptance.

Green is the vibration of relationships, of understanding the needs of others. In a positive, caring relationship, both lives are enriched and expanded and your interaction with the world is broadened. When a relationship is negative or manipulative, your own potential for understanding the world is curtailed and restricted.

▼ THE GREEN OF FRESH HERBS CAN PROMOTE A SENSE OF HARMONY.

◀ GREEN IS THE COLOUR OF THE HEART CHAKRA.

The green personality is prosperous and loves to share what it accumulates. Green may have a conflict of ideas but it always strives to maintain the status quo. Green has the ability to discriminate. Used in a positive manner this can promote tolerance.

GREEN AND THE BODY

The colour green is connected to the shoulders, chest, lower lungs, thymus gland and heart.

▼ PARKS ARE A HAVEN FOR CITY DWELLERS, HELPING THEM APPLY GREEN IN THEIR LIVES.

WHEN GREEN CAN HELP

• Problems with personal relationships, especially when there is a difficulty with over-dominance or subservience, can be helped by green, as can feelings such as envy, jealousy and greed. The desire to dominate or possess is a negative tendency which green can help.
• Claustrophobia or feelings of restriction caused by being housebound or confined, or feelings of being trapped by other people's rules and regulations can be counter-acted by the green vibration.
• Green can restore stability to any situation. It helps to counteract biliousness and a feeling of nausea.

The energy of blue

The colour blue has a stillness about it. It values honour, integrity and sincerity. Blue thinks before acting and proceeds steadily and with caution. It is tranquil and avoids drawing attention to itself.

THE CHARACTER OF BLUE

There are two aspects of blue. One is the process of communication and the flow of energy, and the other is the experience of rest and peacefulness.

Blue is the spirit of truth and higher intelligence. It is spiritually calming, the colour of the writer, poet, and philosopher. The head and the heart speak directly through the blue throat when there is a need to communicate clearly. Honesty and integrity are key blue qualities, and so if blue is lacking, attempts at self-

▲ GAZE AT THE SEA OR THE SKY FOR A NATURAL DOSE OF BLUE. IT WILL INSTIL A SENSE OF PEACE AND TRANQUILLITY.

expression can lead to frustration and disappointment. However, a blue personality that is out of balance can be subtly (or even unconsciously) manipulative. It dislikes upsets and arguments, but may cause them indirectly.

Blue is a cool vibration; it is the tranquil spirit, the colour of contemplation, and it brings rest. It can help to heal inflammations in the body by cooling the area down, and can also help to counteract infection.

This quality of peace gives blue a sense of detachment from emotional turmoil. It is not over-whelmed by closeness or

▼ DIVING IS THE PERFECT PASTIME FOR PEOPLE WITH AN ON-GOING NEED FOR BLUE.

◀ ON A CLEAR SUNNY DAY, BEING ON WATER WILL FILL YOU WITH BLUE ENERGY.

detail, having the possibility of greater perspectives. The blue personality brings a wisdom to love. Blue is also linked to loyalty. This is the quality that can lead you towards the source of devotion.

The sky blue hue encourages a freedom of spirit. It brings solace where cruelty and brutality have occurred. It is a universal healing colour as it constantly creates – and maintains – calm, while overcoming obstacles with no apparent effort.

BLUE AND THE BODY

The colour blue is concerned with the throat area, upper lungs and arms, and the base of the skull. It relates to weight gain. The connected glands are the thyroid and parathyroids. Infections in the throat area are often psychologically related to not speaking out. Since the blue personality hates arguments, it may even resort to coughing and spluttering to avoid any form of confrontation.

WHEN BLUE CAN HELP

• Coughs, sore throats, vocal problems, teething and ear infections can all be treated with blue. A stiff neck, which can represent the fear of moving forwards, also responds. • Blue is particularly useful in reducing the temperature of a fever in adults and children. • Blue can help to calm those who are over-excited or agitated. When used for people with terminal illnesses it can bring a tremendous feeling of peace.

▶ BLUE IS THE COLOUR OF THE THROAT CHAKRA, AND RELATES TO PERSONAL EXPRESSION.

The energy of indigo

Indigo has a strong belief in law and order and a great love of tradition. However, it can also be a transformer, a defender of people's rights, and it has an affinity with a deep inner world.

THE CHARACTER OF INDIGO

The indigo vibration is related to subtle perceptions, such as clairvoyance and other psychic skills. The deep, directionless depths of indigo can heighten our awareness of what is not immediately apparent.

The indigo personality loves structure and hates untidyness. It may ally itself with the Establishment, often upholding the social order in a positive, constructive way. However, a weak indigo personality may become bossy (and over-controlling), or a slave to rigid ideas.

▲ INDIGO PEOPLE WILL OFTEN SEEK SOLITUDE TO DEEPEN THEIR EXPERIENCE OF THE SPIRITUAL OR MYSTICAL REALMS.

When in tune with its inner qualities, the indigo personality can be self-reliant, stepping aside from the world to come up with new ways of thinking. Indigo is an ideal colour for contemplative and spiritual pursuits, such as solitary meditation and visualization, where the inner senses are the most important. Indigo is a stronger philosopher than blue.

The indigo personality may aspire to be a spiritual master, an inspired preacher or writer. Indigo can reconcile science and religion.

◀ GAZE INTO THE INDIGO OF THE MIDNIGHT SKY TO PREPARE FOR THE NEXT STEP IN LIFE.

▶ LIKE A BOLT OF LIGHTNING, INTUITIVE INDIGO REALIZATIONS OFTEN OCCUR ALMOST INSTANTANEOUSLY.

It has a pioneering essence, but pioneers with insight. Negative indigo is the believer who has become a fanatic: blind devotion is an indigo failing. Addictions relate to negative indigo.

The flow of indigo energy creates an internal communication that manifests as profound thought processes, new insights, philosophy and intuition. The indigo vibration enhances and heightens awareness, while maintaining integrity. Stillness and contemplation can lead to a "super-cooled" state of indigo, in which intuition and sudden clarity of understanding can occur. The depths of indigo may seem mysterious, but its influence can yield pertinent information.

INDIGO AND THE BODY

The bone structure, especially the backbone, the pituitary gland, lower brain, eyes and sinuses are all represented by the colour indigo.

◀ THE INDIGO VIBRATION OPENS UP THE "THIRD EYE".

WHEN INDIGO CAN HELP

• Indigo is the strongest painkiller in the spectrum and is a great healer. It can be used to combat many illnesses, among them bacterial infections, and the results of air, water and food pollution.

• Indigo can help acute sinus problems (which psychologically are often uncried tears from childhood), chest complaints, bronchitis and asthma, lumbago, sciatica and migraine. Over-active thyroid, growths, tumours and lumps of any kind, diarrhoea and kidney complaints also respond to the use of indigo.

• The sedative influence of indigo can be helpful in lowering high blood pressure.

• Emotional and mental agitation can also be cooled and quietened by the calming effects of indigo. It is the perfect colour to induce a deep, healing peace.

The energy of purple

Purple can achieve great humility, even to the point of sacrificing itself for the benefit of others, without being a victim. It also has the ability to integrate psychic perception into everyday life.

THE CHARACTER OF PURPLE

The key to understanding the energy of purple is to see how its component colours, red and blue, work together: red is dynamic, while blue is quietening. Purple brings a new dynamism to blue's still qualities, and stability to the frenetic activity of red. Concepts and ideas are thus better able to find some real application. Purple is associated with imagination and psychic inspiration.

There is a danger that purple can become very arrogant. Where this happens inspiration becomes fanaticism and megalomania and imagination turns into fantasy and

▲ PURPLE IS A GREAT PROTECTOR. IT IS RELIABLE AND SOLID, LIKE A HIGH AND MIGHTY MOUNTAIN RANGE.

delusion. The purple energy, because it seems to extend beyond current knowledge into unknown regions, can trap the spiritual dreamer in a world of unrealistic wishful thinking.

If fantasy about the unknown can be avoided, purple energy can bring enlightenment and healing. It integrates energies at all levels, and as healing requires the building up of new systems (red), according to accurate information (blue), so purple energy can accelerate healing, both physical and emotional.

◄ PURPLE ENERGY COMBINES GENTLENESS WITH POWER.

◄ PURPLE IS THE COLOUR OF THE CROWN CHAKRA, WHICH GOVERNS THE BRAIN.

The skill of integration is aided by purple. As the colour combines opposite energies, so it can help people who also need to work with an array of disparate things. It is often associated with the richness and diversity of ceremony, and with rulers and spiritual masters. Clergymen, musicians and painters all work with the colour purple. Humility is a key aspect, but negative purple can be belligerent and treacherous.

PURPLE AND THE BODY
The top of the head – the crown, the brain and the scalp – is represented by purple, as is the pineal gland.

◄ LAVENDER IS A GENTLE BUT VERY POWERFUL HEALER.

WHEN PURPLE CAN HELP
• Purple can be used to treat any kind of internal inflammation, or heart palpitations or headaches. • The immune system and strained nerves can also benefit from the use of purple which enhances the natural healing energy of the body, strengthening the immune system.
• When there is a need to rebalance life, especially if it is lacking in a creative aspect, purple can increase the ability to use the imagination in practical ways and help to integrate new skills into everyday life.
• Purple can calm hyperactive states.

the energy of purple **35**

The energy of black

Black is connected to the secret mystery of darkness. It contains every colour within itself, absorbing all light that falls on it and giving out nothing except a promise. It is linked to unseen, hidden and fearful experiences.

THE CHARACTER OF BLACK

Black is the energy of gestation and of preparation. It has often been associated with winter and with the promise of seeds lying buried and dormant awaiting spring's growth and the new life to come.

Black is the colour of the person who keeps control by not giving information to others. Someone wearing black continuously may be saying that there is something absent from his or her life. Negative black believes that all is ended, there is nothing to look forward to. It is afraid of what is coming next.

When the energy of black is harnessed in a positive way, it can provide the discipline necessary to work through difficul-

▲ THE COLOUR BLACK IS OFTEN SEEN AS NEGATIVE, BUT IT CAN BE THE PRECURSOR OF CHANGE FOR THE BETTER.

ties and achieve freedom. Working towards the light in any way will involve using the magic of black. Black can complete the incomplete. The mystic arts relate to black.

BLACK AND THE BODY

There are no parts of the body specifically connected to black except when seen on X-rays or in the aura as disease.

WHEN BLACK CAN HELP

- Use black in a positive way to encourage self-discipline.
- To break the stagnation of black, a small addition of colour will help the person trapped in black to reach out.

◀ BLACK CLOTHES SUGGEST SELF-DISCIPLINE.

The energy of white

White is what is perceived as the entire visible light spectrum, the complete energy of light, and so it stands for wholeness and completion. White is next to the cosmic intelligence of brilliance – but has a denser brilliance.

THE CHARACTER OF WHITE

Many cultures associate white with purity and cleanliness, openness and truth. It is often used to denote holiness. It reflects all the light that falls on it, thus radiating all the colours of the rainbow.

White's fundamental characteristic is equality: all colours remain equal in white's domain. It is also a symbol of unity and faith. White has a sense of destiny. Everything is clear and explicit. It also has a cold quality. As a vibration of purification, white can help to clarify all

▲ BURNING PURE WHITE CANDLES WILL BRING A PURITY OF THOUGHT AND OPENNESS TO NEW EXPERIENCES IN YOUR LIFE.

aspects of life, giving the energy to sweep away all physical blocks and ingrained emotional patterns.

WHITE AND THE BODY

The eyeball is connected to the colour white: its differing shades of whiteness are used in the diagnosis of illness.

▼ "PURE AS THE DRIVEN SNOW", A PHRASE THAT LINKS THE TWO ASPECTS OF WHITE.

WHEN WHITE CAN HELP
- White has the ability to radiate out all colours, allowing development in any direction, so it is a good choice when you need some impetus.
- Wear white as a tonic to top up the colours in your body's system.

The energy of gold

True gold has a belief in honour among men. It has the gift to release and forgive. Gold is related to the wise old sage. It is warm and sparkling, while its light-reflecting quality brings illumination to the mind and body.

THE CHARACTER OF GOLD

Gold is purity. It is the soul's experience of all that is past. It has access to knowledge and – most important – to knowledge of the self. Gold means "I am". It does not seek, it has already found. From its deep understanding it is able to forgive and let go of the past. It expands the power of love because it trusts completely and has no vice.

Negative gold's conceit is that of privilege and belief in itself as more worthy than others.

▲ THE GOLDEN LIGHT CAST BY THE SUN TURNS THE LANDSCAPE INTO A RICH AND UPLIFTING COLOUR.

It will blow its own trumpet, but true gold respects and appreciates the value of others.

GOLD AND THE BODY

No parts of the body connect with gold, an offshoot of yellow, but it can be seen in auras.

▼ GOLDEN BEACH HOLIDAYS CAN CAPTURE THE TRUE, NOBLE SPIRIT OF GOLD.

WHEN GOLD CAN HELP
• Physical and psychological depressions can be helped by gold as it is uplifting and dissipates negative energy.
• Any kind of digestive irregularity, rheumatism, arthritis, underactive thyroid can all be helped by gold. It will also reduce scars.

The energy of silver

Silver has a bright reflective quality which can create illusions and promote fluidity. It brings freedom from emotional restrictions. It is related to the moon and can light up our path.

THE CHARACTER OF SILVER

Silver is the thread of cosmic intelligence. An invisible silver cord is said to attach humanity to "the other side". It is able to still the emotions and is a great tranquillizer. Silver brings a clarity which helps resolve disputes. It takes an unbiased stand.

Negative silver shows up in relationships in which there is no substance, just delusion. People who fall in love with stars of the silver screen are under this negative influence. Professions that create make-believe also work under silver's influence.

◀ SILVER REPRESENTS ENDURANCE AND IS OFTEN USED FOR TROPHIES.

SILVER AND THE BODY

The feminine dimension of the self is silver, whether it resides in a male or female body. Bathe in the moonlight to restore your equilibrium.

▾ SILVER CUTLERY CAN PROMOTE BALANCED AND FRIENDLY MEALTIME CONVERSATION.

▾ SILVER IS A COLOUR FOR THOSE WHO NEED TO RESOLVE DISPUTES AT WORK.

WHEN SILVER CAN HELP
• Silver brings freedom from emotional restriction: it is the great tranquillizer.
• Silver reflects mistakes without distortion. It harmonizes and brings about a fluid state of consciousness.

The energy of turquoise and pink

Turquoise combines the calming, balancing qualities of green and the cool, quiet flow of blue with the warmth of yellow. Pink is also a blend, combining red and white. This mixture promotes consistency of affection.

THE CHARACTER OF TURQUOISE

In the body, turquoise is related to the throat and chest. The energy of turquoise allows self-expression, as the green quality of growth is added to the blue quality of communication, while the yellow explores information through feelings and emotions. A wonderful healing colour for the central nervous system, turquoise is a colour that allows you to stand still for a while and think only of yourself. The turquoise personality's basic motivation is to seek self-fulfilment in a personal relationship.

WHEN TURQUOISE CAN HELP
• When the throat and chest need soothing, there is low energy, or a failure to fit in, turquoise can help.

WHEN PINK CAN HELP
• In any turbulent or aggressive situation, pink can help to calm violent emotions and it will provide energy to move out of a negative situation.

THE CHARACTER OF PINK

The quality of pink energy depends on how much red is present. White stands for equality, red is the motivation to achieve a goal. Pink represents caring and tenderness and a limited exposure to pink can temper aggressive behaviour. The richer shades can help to improve self-confidence and assertiveness while the paler shades are more protective and supportive.

◄ PLACE THE COLOURED CRYSTAL OR STONE NEAR THE AREA THAT REQUIRES HEALING.

The energy of brown and grey

Brown is a colour of the earth and the natural world. It is the colour of solidity, preferring not to take risks. Grey is the true neutral colour, the bridge between white and black, where innocence and ignorance meet.

THE CHARACTER OF BROWN

Brown is a colour of practical energy. The brown personality is a deep thinker and can be very single-minded.

Like black, brown represents the seed waiting patiently to develop its full potential. It is the colour of hibernation. It suggests reliability and a state of solidity from which one can grow. Brown can suggest a quiet desire to remain in the background. However, it can also have a dulling effect as it lacks the ability to break out of established patterns. A touch of brown in a room can be warmly comforting.

▲ ▼ THE DARK GREY OF THE MOUNTAIN, ABOVE, GIVES IT A FORBIDDING QUALITY, WHEREAS THE LIGHT GREY OF THE MOUNTAINS, BELOW, HAS AN ETHEREAL FEELING.

THE CHARACTER OF GREY

When grey contains a high proportion of white it tends to take on the qualities of silver's flow, but darker grey can be draining as the black in it can cause depression. However, grey can also help you to break free from the chains that bind. Negative grey is conventional to the point of narrow-mindedness. When the skin and nails have a grey tint, this can indicate congestion somewhere in the body.

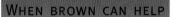

WHEN BROWN CAN HELP
• Brown is a neutral and non-threatening colour which begets comfort and stability.

WHEN GREY CAN HELP
• Grey is not commonly used in healing, but light grey is extremely soothing.

Hidden colours

All colours, apart from the rainbow hues, are combinations of other colours. When using colour for healing, it is important to remember that these hidden colours will have a subtle effect that can be beneficial.

Colour components

When you are working with colour – particularly when you are using it for healing – it is important to be aware of what are known as hidden colours. For instance, orange is made up of the hidden colours of red and yellow. The eye will see orange but the body will also experience the red and yellow vibrations that are within the orange. Therefore, when working with orange for healing, you should take account of the psychological effects of red and yellow as well as those of orange.

The colour green has its own healing meaning, and also the meaning of the yellow and blue

◀ Orange flowers also radiate the solo energies of red and yellow.

rays that make up green. Turquoise is a combination of all three of these rays. Similarly, purple has red and blue within it, so remember to evaluate these colour effects too. Grey, of course, consists of the hidden colours black and white. Brown is made up of various colours including yellow, red, and even black. Like all colours, brown has a wide range of shades or tints, each with a differing effect in healing. Every shade or tint has a unique combination of hidden colours.

◀ GREEN'S HEALING QUALITY INCLUDES THE EFFECTS OF YELLOW AND BLUE

Complementary colours

Every colour of the spectrum has an opposite colour that complements it. Knowing these complementary colours will help you to identify which colours you need for healing, support and help.

OPPOSITES

The complementary colour of red is blue, that of orange is indigo and yellow's is purple. Green, the middle colour of the rainbow, has magenta, which is made up of red and blue.

A knowledge of complementary colours is often useful in everyday life. For example, if you feel extremely irritated by someone's behaviour, you will be reacting to an overload of red vibration within your system. To counteract this, just think of blue, put on some blue clothing or gaze at any blue object. Continue until you feel the anger pass. Or

▶ ALL COLOURS OF THE SPECTRUM HAVE A COMPLEMENTARY COLOUR. GREEN'S IS MAGENTA, AN EXTRA COLOUR MADE UP OF RED AND BLUE.

you may find yourself in a room with yellow decor that you find disturbing. Close your eyes and conjure up the colour purple – the complementary of yellow – to dispel the yellow vibration.

An understanding of complementary colours can be helpful when you are using a lamp with coloured slides for healing. Use a blue slide to relieve the red of irritability, for instance, or a red slide to pull you out of the blues. If you are ever in doubt about a colour, or have a feeling that too much colour has been used, just flood yourself with green light or visualize it. Green acts as a neutralizer, returning balance and order to any situation.

◀ WEARING THE COMPLEMENTARY COLOURS RED AND BLUE CAN HAVE A POSITIVE EFFECT.

Hues, tints and shades

The description of a colour usually refers to the hue, that is one of the colours of the rainbow. Each colour can vary, it may be light or dark. These variations can be extremely beneficial when used for healing.

LIGHT AND DARK HUES

All variations of a hue share its underlying qualities, but their psychological meanings are modified according to whether they are a higher (tint) or lower (shade) tone. Tints are paler (higher) colours which have more white in them. This gives them a stronger healing quality. For example, the white added to red to create pink brings with it a compassionate and spiritual quality. The paler the pink, the greater the healing qualities it

▲ THE RAINBOW CONTAINS THE SEVEN HUES USED IN COLOUR HEALING: RED, ORANGE, YELLOW, GREEN, BLUE, INDIGO AND PURPLE.

possesses. Shades of a colour are darker (lower) and are produced when the basic hue is mixed with black.

In general, the tints are considered positive and the shades negative. But this can be misleading as the darker shades can alert you to problems that you may need to address.

▼ WEARING A PALE TINT OF PINK CAN BRING A STRONG SENSE OF CALM.

COLOUR DEFINITIONS

Hue: a basic colour in the visible spectrum, a ray

Tint: a hue plus white

Shade: a hue plus black

Colour categories

Colours can be grouped into practical categories, based upon the four elements (fire, earth, air and water) and the seasons. These colour groupings relate to personality types, and most people are drawn to one particular group.

COLOUR PREFERENCE

A colour grouping can help in your choice of colours for home decorations, clothes and belongings. You may be drawn to more than one category, which can be useful if you have to compromise with other people over room décor.

Occasionally, your second preference can be useful if you are choosing clothes to create a particular image for a specific purpose, but wearing colours to impress others may feel uncomfortable compared to wearing your natural, instinctive choice.

SPRING – WATER

Warm, light tints: turquoise, lilac, peach, coral, scarlet, violet, emerald, sunshine yellow, cream, sand.
Clear, almost delicate colours, that create a joyful and nurturing ambience.

SUMMER – AIR

Subtle tones, some dark, containing grey: maroon, rose, powder blue, sage green, pale yellow, lavender, plum, oyster, taupe.
Colours that are elegant, cool and contained, never heavy.

AUTUMN – FIRE

Warm shades (containing some black): mustard, olive green, flame, peacock, burnt orange, teal, burgundy.
Very rich, striking colours that suggest maturity and depth.

WINTER – EARTH

Sharp contrasts between hues, tints and shades: black, white, magenta, cyan, purple, lemon, silver, indigo, royal blue, jade.
Bold and powerful colours, with no subtlety.

Choosing colours

Your instinctive emotional response to colour can tell you a lot about yourself. It is possible to interpret your colour preferences through their known correspondences to your physical, emotional, mental and even your spiritual state.

SIMPLE CHOICE

Given a number of colours to choose from, the process of self-reflection and self-revelation can begin. The simplest approach is to make spontaneous choices. Which colour do you like most, and which colour the least?

The colour you like most will probably be evident in the way you have decorated your home or in your clothes. But it may also be a colour that you need now to help support you in your present situation. Look at the full range of characteristics of that colour for

▲ YOUR CHOICE OF FLOWERS FOR THE GARDEN MAY REVEAL TENDENCIES TOWARDS CERTAIN COLOURS.

clues to other aspects that may help. If the colour you have chosen is an absolute favourite and you have no desire to make other choices, it could indicate that you have become stuck in a habitual pattern.

The colour you like least could suggest an area of your life that requires attention or healing. Bringing that colour energy into your life by adding it to your surroundings may be beneficial.

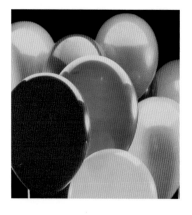

◀ A CHILD'S CHOICE OF BALLOON MAY GIVE YOU INSIGHT INTO THEIR MENTAL STATE.

Multiple choice

The process can be developed by making a series of choices. Decide beforehand what question each choice will represent. For example:

1 What are your physical needs now (activities, food, clothing)?

2 What are your emotional needs now (peace, fun, company)?

3 What are your mental needs now (time to study, assertiveness)?

How to do it

1 Use the chart overleaf, or collect together ribbons or buttons, at least one of each colour of the rainbow, plus a few other colours.

2 Lay them out at random on a plain background.

3 Close your eyes and have in your mind the first question.

4 Relax, open your eyes and pick up the colour you are immediately and instinctively drawn to.

5 Repeat the process for each question you ask.

Interpreting your choices

Look at your colour choice for each question and relate it to the meaning of that colour. You can then introduce the energy of the colour into your everyday life.

▲ A simple collection of different coloured fabrics can be useful for diagnosing the necessary colours.

Taking it further

You can invent any number of permutations for a series of questions. Here is just one possible list:

1 Where am I now?

2 What are my main difficulties?

3 What is at the root of those difficulties?

4 What are my priority needs?

5 What is the best way for me to move forwards?

▼ Make colour choices in your own mind, simply imagine them and choose.

Using a colour-choice chart

You can use this colour chart to help you with your self-assessment or make your own chart using different paints or pieces of cloth. If you make your own you will be able to include as many colours as you like.

USING THE CHART

Before you begin to choose your colours, cover the meanings with a sheet of paper. This will help stop your eyes scanning the other page and will prevent the logical and judgemental part of your mind from interfering with your instinctive choice of colour.

Decide how many choices you will make and what each will represent, then close your eyes. For each choice, consider the question you are asking then open your eyes and see which colour you are immediately drawn to.

Record the colour you choose for each question. When you have made all your choices, remove the paper and study the key phrases and questions in the interpretation chart to help you focus your ideas. Where appropriate, introduce more of the colours you have chosen into your life, whether in terms of food, decor or clothing.

COLOUR-CHOICE CHART

DARK RED · RED · ORANGE · GOLD · YELLOW · OLIVE GREEN

GREEN · TURQUOISE · LIGHT BLUE · DARK BLUE · PURPLE · BLACK

WHITE · PINK · MAGENTA · SILVER · BROWN · GREY

Colour Chart Interpretations

Dark red
You need to keep your feet firmly on the ground. What is taking your attention away from where it needs to be?

Red
You need to take action, now. What is stopping you?

Orange
You need to let go of old emotions and ideas. What are you allowing to block your way?

Gold
You need to relax and enjoy life. What is it that is making you doubt yourself?

Yellow
You need to start thinking clearly. What are you afraid of?

Olive green
You need to reassess where you are going. What hidden factors are stopping your growth?

Green
You need space to gain a fresh perspective. What is it that is restricting you?

Turquoise
You need to express exactly what you feel. What are your strengths?

Light blue
You need to talk to people around you. What do you need to express to others?

Dark blue
You need time to think. What are you so close to that you cannot see clearly what is happening?

Purple
You need to heal yourself. What are you sacrificing to help others?

Black
You need to be quiet and listen. What do you want to hide from?

White
You need to make changes. What do you find painful in the real world?

Pink
You need to look after yourself more. Are you being too self-critical?

Magenta
You need to take time out to heal yourself. Are you risking your own health by overdoing things?

Silver
You need to restore your equilibrium. What are you deluding yourself about?

Brown
You need to focus on practicalities. What areas of your life have you been too dreamy about?

Grey
You need to disappear into the background. What do you want to hide and why?

Colour and food

The colour of the foods we eat can have a powerful effect on our physical and emotional state. Eating the appropriate coloured foods can help to rejuvenate and balance the system, making you feel brighter and more alive.

FRESH FOODS

Wholesome, fresh food is full of colour energy. Seek out foods that are organically grown with no additives, as this will keep the colour vibration alive. Become aware of the colours of the different foods you choose, as your preferences can convey valuable information about yourself.

Your body will normally direct you to the foods that you need to rebalance your health, though habit or advertising may intrude on what should be an important guide for your health. Given a free choice, you will always tend to be drawn to those foods you need, and colour is an important factor.

If you have problems that correspond to certain colours you may wish to increase foods of that colour in your diet. Nutrients such as vitamins and minerals also resonate with particular colours, and these are included in the following lists, as are "non-foods" (foods with little nutritional value) which you may also crave at times when you need instant energy.

▸ RED FOODS PROMOTE TIRELESS ENERGY AND LIVELY ACTION.

FOOD COLOURS
Red: Gives extra energy, heals lethargy and tiredness
Orange: Creates optimism and change, heals grief and disappointment
Yellow: Encourages laughter, joy and fun, heals depression
Green: Improves physical stamina, heals panic
Blue: Brings peace and relaxation, helps concentration and heals anxiety
Indigo: Puts back structure into life, heals insecurity
Purple: Promotes leadership, heals and calms the emotionally erratic

Red foods and orange foods

RED FOODS

Foods that are red in colour are generally rich in minerals and are good sources of protein. They increase levels of vitality. Red deficiencies are shown through low energy, anaemia, light-headedness and lack of stamina. Red foods can also help heart problems of an emotional or physical nature. However, professional medical advice should also be sought.

FOOD FACTS

Fruits: strawberries, raspberries, cherries

Vegetables: red cabbage, beetroot, radishes, peppers (also green, orange and yellow), onions, tomatoes

Other foods: meat, pulses, nuts, fish

Vitamins: B12

Minerals: iron, magnesium, zinc (also orange)

Other nutrients: fatty acids

Non-foods: sugar (also yellow and purple)

ORANGE FOODS

The release of toxins and stress from the body is associated with orange. It also supports the reproductive system and encourages creativity on all levels: orange may help with writer's block. Vitamin C and zinc both resonate with orange and provide an excellent detoxifying combination to help the body rid itself of heavy metals and other pollutants. A lack of orange will often cause problems in the area of the orange chakra such as constipation or fertility problems, and also stiffness in the joints.

FOOD FACTS

Fruits: oranges, peaches, apricots, physalis, kumquats, persimmon

Vegetables: pumpkin, peppers (also green, red and yellow), carrots

Other foods: brown rice, sesame, oats, shellfish

Vitamins: A, C

Minerals: calcium, copper, selenium, zinc (also red)

Yellow foods and green foods

YELLOW FOODS
The sun is the main source of yellow during daylight hours, but most people work indoors and modern life uses up the yellow vibration dealing with pollution, chemicals, and high stress levels. Yellow foods can help. Lack of yellow leads to exhaustion, tension, restlessness, poor absorption of nutrients, digestive problems, lowered immunity, hot flushes, depression, poor memory and inability to make decisions.

GREEN FOODS
The foods that are of a green nature tend to be very rich in vitamins and minerals, though these can be lost in cooking or storage, so eat lots of fresh fruit and salad. Growing your own vegetables is a great way to ensure their freshness, as well as bringing you in touch with nature. Lack of green vibration creates an inability to relate, a feeling of being trapped, breathing difficulties and negative emotions.

FOOD FACTS

Fruits: lemon, bananas, grapefruit

Vegetables: grains, peppers, squash

Other foods: eggs, fish, oils, food rich in fatty acids

Vitamins and minerals: A, B complex, D, E, sodium potassium, selenium (also orange), phosphorus, iodine (also blue), chromium, molybdenite, manganese

Non-foods: food additives, alcohol, sugar (also red and purple)

FOOD FACTS

Fruits: apples, pears, avocado, green grapes, lime, kiwi fruits

Vegetables: cabbage, calabrese, broccoli, kale, sprouts, green beans, peas, leeks, other dark green leafy vegetables

Other: most culinary herbs – marjoram, basil, oregano, parsley

Vitamins and minerals: all vitamins, no minerals

▶ EAT PLENTY OF FRESH GREENS.

Blue and purple foods

BLUE AND PURPLE FOODS

Very few foods are naturally coloured blue or purple, but several work with a blue or purple vibration. Blue foods are useful when the voice and communication skills, glands or organs of the neck need a helping hand. Purple vibration foods can have a remarkable effect on the workings of the mind. Small amounts of basil, can help to relax the body while keeping the mind alert.

OTHER WORLDS, OTHER FOODS

Some foods with a purple resonance have long been used in healing. Used carefully, they can open the consciousness to other realms of experience and possibilities. In Central America the peyote cactus (*Lophophora williamsii*) is ritually harvested and used in religious and healing ceremonies, and ayahuasca (*Banesteriopsis caapi*) is collected throughout the Amazon basin for a similar purpose. Both are well known as purifiers of the body and can remove the causes of illness. The herb variety called holy basil is kept by many in the Indian subcontinent as a sacred herb of meditation.

◀ BLUE AND PURPLE FOODS OPEN THE MIND TO OTHER WORLDS.

FOOD FACTS

Fruits: plums, blueberries, black grapes, figs, passion fruit

Blue vibration vegetables: kelp and all seaweed products

Purple vegetables: purple sprouting broccoli, aubergines

Purple vibration plants: St John's wort

Vitamins: E

Blue minerals: iodine
Purple minerals: potassium

Non-foods: food additives and colourings, alcohol, sugar (also red)

Healing with coloured light

The human species has evolved to be reactive to sunlight, so living and working indoors, often under artificial lighting, may be an important factor in undermining health. Coloured light can counteract some of these harmful effects.

SEASONAL AFFECTIVE DISORDER
Studies of plants have demonstrated that full-spectrum natural sunlight, including ultraviolet (filltered out by most types of glass), plays an important part in maintaining the healthy functioning of plants and animals. The lack of sunlight in winter can be debilitating, and people can suffer from a condition known as Seasonal Affective Disorder (SAD), with accompanying mood swings and low energy, when levels of the hormone-like melatonin are reduced in the body. The condition can be treated with several hours daily of bright full-spectrum light.

▲ YOU CAN USE CHROMOTHERAPY ON SPECIFIC AREAS.

CHROMOTHERAPY
On a basic level, chromotherapy, or light treatment, works by using different coloured gels or slides in front of high-powered lamps to bathe either the whole body or specific problem areas. The application of different coloured lights can bring about relief both for the body and spirit. The recipient of the treatment can either lie down or sit in a chair, with the lamp directed towards them. For any serious illness, however, you should always consult a medical practitioner.

◄ USE COLOURED GELS IN FRONT OF A SPOTLIGHT TO CREATE HEALING COLOURED LIGHT.

COLOURED LIGHTING

By installing a lighting system that enables you to turn on any colour at will, you can flood the room with your chosen colour. This enables you to be bathed in a colour treatment for maximum health and well-being.

You can achieve the same effect very easily by acquiring a free-standing spotlight and selecting a coloured slide or gel appropriate to your needs. Place the gel over the spotlight, taking care to ensure it is not touching the hot bulb. Turn off any other lights in the room and turn on the spotlight. Sit with the spotlight shining on you and bathe in the coloured light for an instantly available, on-the-spot therapy.

▲ PINK COUNTERACTS AN OVERLOAD OF WHITE, SO PINK FLOWERS ARE COMFORTING WHEN GIVEN TO SOMEONE IN HOSPITAL.

THE ALL-WHITE ROOM

The perfect healing sanctuary for chromotherapy will be a white room. However, an all-white room in an everyday situation will cause an overload of white; if you are surrounded by it for too long it can cause agitation and frustration. Placing one red object in the room, or arranging flowers of the same hue, will dissipate the sterility that too much white can cause. You can help friends or relatives staying in all-white hospital rooms by taking in appropriately coloured flowers. Blue can help to calm fear and pre-operative nerves, while peach and pink introduce a little stimulation when the patient is recovering.

◄ SATURATE YOURSELF IN THE CALMING BLUE RAY FOR PEACE AND TRANQUILLITY.

Colour essences

Colour essences are vibrational remedies. They contain nothing other than water which has been energized by the action of natural sunlight passing through a coloured filter. They are easy to make and effect

How colour essences work

Some of the pioneers of colour therapy theorized that the atomic structure of the water was somehow altered and given particular life-enhancing proper-ties. Current medical research is slowly coming to a very similar conclusion and is developing techniques to target specific light frequencies on diseased tissue to restore normal functioning to the cells. Vibrational remedies seem to work by helping the body to return to its natural state of balance after any kind of stress or shock has disturbed it.

▼ Colour essences can be stored for a few weeks in brown glass bottles.

▶ Save scraps of coloured cloth to make colour essences.

Although very simple to make, colour essences can be very effective tools for healing. Rapid release of stress can sometimes feel uncomfort-able, and if this is experienced, simply reduce the amount, or stop using the essence for a day or two. Taking essences last thing at night, and then sleeping while they take effect, is a good way to comfortably restore a state of balance. They can also be taken first thing in the morning, which is a good way to make them part of your daily routine, but you may find that you need to take a bit more time getting up, if they affect you strongly.

Like all vibrational remedies, they have the advantage of being self-regulating: the body will only make use of the energy within the essence if it is appropriate.

Using essences

Colour essences can be used in many ways. A little can be drunk each day in water, or if you place an essence in a dropper bottle, it can be dropped directly on to the tongue. Because they are purely vibrational in nature, the colour essences only need to be within the energy field of the body to begin working, so other methods can also be used. You can spray it around your body for immediate effect; drop a little on to the pulse points at your wrists, the side of your neck or your forehead; rub it on to the area needing help or the related chakra point; or add a drop or two to bathwater or massage oil.

Healing colour essence

You will need
Plain glass bottle or bowl
Spring water
Coloured gel or other thin coloured material
Brown glass storage bottle
Label
Preservative, such as alcohol, cider vinegar, honey or vegetable glycerine

1 Fill the bottle or bowl with spring water and cover completely with a coloured gel or cloth. You can also use a sheet of coloured glass laid over a bowl, but the essence will be most effective if only coloured light enters the water.

2 Leave the bowl or glass in bright natural sunlight for at least two hours.

3 If you wish to keep the essence for future use, make a 50/50 mix of energized water and preservative, such as alcohol, cider vinegar or vegetable glycerine. It should be kept in a brown bottle away from light. It will keep in this way for many months.

Flowers and colour

For thousands of years plants have been used by different cultures to help to keep the body healthy and to fight disease. Many herbs indicate by their colour and shape how they can be used in healing.

FLOWER ESSENCES

Paracelsus, the 16th-century Swiss physician and occultist, is believed to have used the dew of flowers for healing and there is some evidence that flower waters were also an integral part of Tibetan medical practices. More recently, in the 20th century, Dr Bach rediscovered the healing properties of flower essences.

Colour flower essences are made by placing flowers in a bowl of water and energizing it with sunlight. As before, use flowers that you are instinctively drawn to.

Red flowers often boost energy levels. The flower essence of scarlet pimpernel (*Anagallis arvensis*), for example, can help to activate energy and clear deep-seated blocks. The elm *(Ulmus procera)* has deep red and purple flowers, and the flower essence helps to clear the mind when fatigue and confusion have set in. In this case, the red stimulates the energy reserves and the purple balances the mind.

Blue flowers will often bring a sense of peace and help with communication and expression. For example, the forget-me-not (*Myosotis arvensis*), as a flower essence, can aid memory and help those who feel cut off from deeper

▾ YOU CAN USE YOUR INTUITION TO CHOOSE PLANTS FOR FLOWER ESSENCES.

levels of experience. Sage (*Salvia officinalis*) has violet-blue flowers that suggest it would be effective in the areas of the head and throat. The flower essence helps to give a broader outlook on life and a balance to the mind, encouraging the exploration of ideas.

Yellow flowers bring optimism and help to release tensions. The flower essence of dandelion (*Taraxacum officinale*) is a muscle relaxant which can also help to release rigid mental belief systems. The way in which the seeds disperse at the slightest breeze can be seen as a symbol of the quality of letting go.

Pink flowers are some of the most powerful healers, and there are many to choose from, including the pink *(Dianthus)*, the rose (*Rosa damascena*), and the chive flower *(Allium schoenoprasum)*. Pink can help to counteract aggressive behaviour and it also encourages the qualities of generosity and affection.

Since white contains all the colours of the spectrum, white flower essences act generally, giving the body an overall boost. Common elder *(Sambucus nigra)* and chamomile *(Chamaemelum nobile)* are both useful flowers.

Although simple to make, colour flower essences can cause rapid release of stress, which can sometimes feel uncomfortable. If this is experienced, simply stop taking the remedy for a day or two or halve the dose from 6 to 3 drops a day.

▼ ST JOHN'S WORT IS AN EFFECTIVE TREATMENT FOR DEPRESSION AND MOODINESS.

Crystals and colour

The key qualities of a colour make it easy to identify how a crystal will interact with human energy systems. Crystals are coherent, organized forms of matter, so the colour they transmit is a very focused, powerful vibration.

HEALING WITH CRYSTALS

The colour of a crystal, whatever its other properties, has a direct effect on you via your eyes and by its placement on different parts of your body. In ancient times, crystals were chosen for their colour content. The chosen-coloured crystal was then crushed into a powder to use as a medication for healing various ailments. Crystals are especially useful for healing emotional problems.

Any crystal, if you are drawn to it, will have a healing effect. If you want help with a specific problem, select a few stones of different colours and work with those you are attracted to, in the same way that you chose colours from the chart.

◄ FOCUS ON A CRYSTAL TO CENTRE YOURSELF AND PROMOTE HEALING.

RED STONES

These stones are energizing and stimulating. Rich, bright reds, like pyrope garnet, ruby and zircon, can be dramatic in their effects. The opaque or brown reds of jasper and iron quartz create a more grounded, practical energy.

ORANGE STONES

These coloured crystals energize the repair mechanisms within the body and are excellent for shock and trauma. Carnelian and orange calcite invigorate and restore, while topaz helps to strengthen and re-integrate dissipated energies.

YELLOW STONES

The yellow of these stones energizes the solar plexus. Citrine, yellow fluorite and amber can promote clarity and self-confidence. Tiger's eye brings wisdom and trust.

GREEN STONES

The emotions and heart are calmed by green crystals. Green aventurine and green tourmaline are good emotional stabilizers. Malachite and dioptase help in coping with emotional pain. Emerald encourages harmonious relationships while peridot lifts the heart.

LIGHT BLUE STONES

The crystal vibration of light blue lace agate and celestite releases tensions and lifts heavy moods. It also inspires ambition and supports communication. Aquamarine and turquoise encourage flexibility as well as enhancing the central nervous system.

DARK BLUE STONES

Dark lapis lazuli and sapphire quieten the normal thought processes, encouraging intuition. Sodalite and kyanite can help to release long-held stresses, encouraging deep peace.

PURPLE STONES,

Like amethyst, fluorite and sugilite make excellent stones for meditation and contemplation. They encourage vision and psychic perception.

BLACK STONES

Like obsidian, smoky quartz, black tourmaline and haematite can help to encourage self-discipline. They also act as a reminder to the heart that there is light at the end of the tunnel.

PINK STONES

Pink stones give a sense of deep affection and love. Rose quartz, rhodocrosite and rhodonite give comfort and can help counter aggression, while kunzite improves the immune system.

COLOURLESS STONES

White and clear stones amplify life-sustaining qualities and bring clarity and order. Clear quartz energizes, while moonstone, milky quartz and other translucent white stones have a cleansing effect.

Meditation and visualization

Colour is a powerful tool in meditation because it has a profound effect on the nervous system, no matter what else may be happening in the mind. Meditating helps you to gather your scattered energies.

CELESTIAL HEALING RAYS

1 Close your eyes and visualize yourself sitting in a grassy, flower-sprinkled meadow with a cool and crystal clear stream running by you. The day is clear and bright, the sky is blue, with a scattering of soft white clouds and birds are singing in the trees.

2 Choose a colour that you need for your personal healing and wellbeing. Next, choose one of the clouds in the sky above you. Let this special cloud become filled with your chosen colour and start to shimmer with its coloured, sparkling light.

3 Allow the cloud to float over you; as it does, visualize the release of a shower of coloured stars cascading in all directions.

4 The mist settles on your skin and it gently becomes absorbed through your skin, saturating your system with its healing vibration.

5 Allow the colour to run through your body and bloodstream for a few minutes, giving your body a therapeutic tonic wash.

6 Allow the pores of your skin to open so that the coloured vapour can escape, taking any toxins with it. When the vapour runs clear, you can close your pores.

7 Stay quietly with your cleared, healed body and mind for a few minutes. Take in three slow and deep breaths, before slowly opening your eyes.

◀ MEDITATE OUT OF DOORS TO RECEIVE THE CALM OF GREEN.

Intuiting colour

You can use colour as a means of tapping into your intuition and developing your psychic ability. This is a sensitivity everyone has, and you can access it simply by making yourself available and clear of mind.

DOWSING WITH CRYSTALS

Use a crystal pendulum. Hold the chain between your first finger and thumb, with the crystal over the palm of your other hand. Ask the pendulum a question. If it swings round to the right the answer is "yes". Swinging to the left means "no". If it swings backwards and forwards the answer is inconclusive.

You can use crystals of different colours for different questions. For instance, if you are asking about relationships, use turquoise; for business and finance, use green.

▸ HOLD THE PENDULUM AND OPEN YOUR MIND; TRY NOT TO GUESS WHAT THE ANSWER MAY BE.

USING A COLOUR WHEEL

Draw a circle on white paper and divide it into as many coloured sections as you wish. Hold a pendulum in the centre of the wheel and ask a question. Allow the pendulum to swing towards whichever colour it wants, to give you psychic colour clues. Refer to the profile of your chosen colour to analyse the information.

Remember that any intuitive process can give only indications as to the correct path you need to take. The art is in the interpretation. Monitor your findings – you will be surprised at how many of them materialize.

◂ DOWSING IS A MEANS OF TAPPING INTO YOUR PSYCHIC ABILITY.

Index